THE
DEAD CAT
BOUNCE

Make Money Fast

Explore the environment of a severe stock market decline and discover how to increase your wealth.

BILL OVERMYER

iUniverse LLC
Bloomington

THE DEAD CAT BOUNCE
Make Money Fast

Front cover art by Bill Overmyer
Back cover art by Bill Overmyer

iUniverse books may be ordered through booksellers or by contacting:

iUniverse
1663 Liberty Drive
Bloomington, IN 47403
www.iuniverse.com
1-800-Authors (1-800-288-4677)

Because of the dynamic nature of the Internet, any web addresses or links contained in this book may have changed since publication and may no longer be valid. The views expressed in this work are solely those of the author and do not necessarily reflect the views of the publisher, and the publisher hereby disclaims any responsibility for them.

This method of investing (buy disaster) has been used successfully by many investors over the last 70 years. It is not fool proof as the timing of the stock purchase and the choice of the company selected will determine the reader's success. The author can not be held liable for bad selection or timing on the part of the reader.

ISBN: 978-1-4759-9875-7 (sc)
ISBN: 978-1-4759-9876-4 (e)

Library of Congress Control Number: 2013912539

Printed in the United States of America.

iUniverse rev. date: 8/30/2013

ACKNOWLEDGEMENTS

Securities Research Company (SRC) grants permission for their charts to be used in this publication. The views expressed in this publication are solely the view of the author and do not reflect the views of SRC. SRC hereby disclaims any responsibility for any content within this publication. Photo copy or reproduction of any material (SRC charts) within this publication by any means and without prior approval and written consent by SRC is prohibited and punishable by law.

Please visit www.srcstockcharts.com.

CONTENTS

APPENDIX

INTRODUCTION

So where do you start? You have expressed an interest and curiosity as you have made it to this page. Here is what you can expect when you finish this book.

You will possess the knowledge and the insight to conduct timely and successful *fire sale shopping* in the stock market. Fire sale shopping is an opportunity to increase your bank account in a short period of time with little or no risk. If you are successful with the *"buy disaster"* concept presented in this book you may become your own boss. You may become financially independent.

This book will show you when to buy stocks in good companies that have dropped drastically in share price during **a steep stock market decline. This is when you buy!** It will be the fastest return on an investment that you will ever see. It will help you pay off your bills and your credit cards. It will give you extra money for yourself. Eventually, it will help you pay down your mortgage or pay it off completely.

The theme of this book describes the environment of a stock market disaster to you. The purpose of the book is to *allow you to enter this atmosphere and buy stocks close to their lowest prices in years*.

This easily understood read will prove that **the Dead Cat Bounce is absolutely the best time and the safest time to profit in the market.** Invest anywhere from $20,000.00 to $50,000.00 or more with very little risk.

There is no uncertainty and there is no guess work. You only have to do your shopping once every four or five years. You only need to have cash available and to be focused when the time is right.

You will be *a winner!*

Now to whet your appetite and get the juices flowing, let us have some fun in the next ten pages with a Dead Cat Bounce scenario.

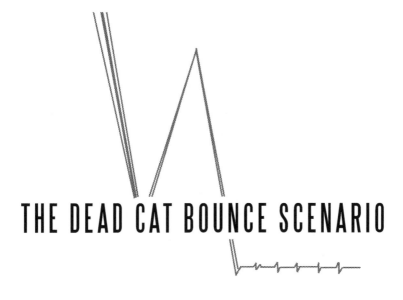

THE DEAD CAT BOUNCE SCENARIO

In the fall of 2007 the Dow Jones Industrial Average index (DJIA) was trading at 14000. The market began to drop in 2008. In October, 2008, the stock market took some steep declines. As of March, 2009, the DJIA index had dropped over fifty percent to 6500. This was the low point for the DJIA index. In the nine months from October, 2008 to June, 2009, a multitude of corporate stocks would drop to the lowest share prices seen in the last twelve years.

Disaster day is here. You need to be in your strategy room more frequently. Signs are ominous. You have been watching your favorite stocks and you are also looking for a **new tide of disaster candidates.** The bad economy has sent share prices into the cellar. Stocks are the last thing anyone wants to buy.

The media has been moaning about the bad condition of the nation's economy every day for the last year. This is now the **third quarter in a row of negative corporate earnings** (three months in a quarter of a year). No one is making any money except for a few well heeled manufacturers. Companies are showing a loss on the bottom line of their income statements. The same situation is the case for the nation's gross domestic production (GDP). The GDP is the lowest it has been in the last four or five years. The economy is shrinking.

Everyone says, "Oh, my God! We are in a recession!" It is a recession. Two full quarters in a row of no growth, no earnings and no profit is the definition of a mild recession. Three quarters in a row of no growth with **negative earnings/income** instead of profits is a real, "Gosh, darn for certain recession."

The four year oil price hike jihad in the Middle East has begun to soak up the profit in the monthly paycheck. You can count on this recurring Jihad. It will happen again. But you are not afraid! You realize that the market will drop when the price of a barrel of oil goes through the roof. You watch the market. You are focused and ready to strike when the time is right.

There are casualties in the stock markets. Some companies that are struggling to limit losses are down fifty percent in share price. Strong companies that still show good profits are down thirty to forty percent in share price. This is not quite the bottom but we are definitely on the way. We are half way there.

As the economy slows the nation "tightens the belt." Companies that experience losses in sales and revenues cut back on production and expenses. Reduced wages for employees means reduced consumer spending from those employees. If the recession continues, then some companies will have layoffs and plant closures as production drops and sales and revenues decline. Many companies will go out of business.

In order to raise cash to survive, Americans and people around the world are selling their rusting all terrain vehicle, jet ski, sail boat, fishing boat, second car, vacation home or plot of land. Consumers default on loans, credit cards and home mortgages. They file for bankruptcy. In six more months foreclosures begin to appear across the country and around the world.

Workers who experience a lay off or a cut in salary will try to hold everything together by refinancing the house and by taking a job with lower pay.

You notice that the banks and the financial companies have taken a huge hit. There is an ocean of stocks that no one wants. One by one, but not all on the same day these stocks will sink to the bottom over a period of nine months. Fannie Mae in December, 2008. Ford in July, 2009. Some will dwell lifelessly on the bottom for a longer period than others.

You are not deterred. The financial sector comes crashing down and with it the DJIA index. It comes down so hard and fast that you duck by reflex. The banks are in trouble due to the home loan and commercial loan foreclosures.

You remain focused. You identify companies with the largest drop in share prices and log them onto your watch list. There are stocks down to five dollars a share from highs of thirty and sixty dollars a share. Bank of America (BAC is the exchange stock symbol) is $2.50. Just a year ago Bank of America traded at $40 to $50 a share for three years.

Huntington Bank (HUNB) is $1.50 down from $60. Huntington Bank traded at $50 a share for four years just a year and a half ago.

Starbucks Coffee Shops (SBUX) is $6 down from $34. CitiGroup (C) is $3. A year and a half ago CitiGroup traded at $55.

The thirty companies that make up the DJIA index were at their low point in March, 2009. The 3,100 companies (approximate number) on the NASDAQ and the other 2800 companies (approximate number) from the NYSE will take their turns for their individual low point one day at a time.

You are focused on your five favorite stocks and you monitor their bid and ask windows. You watch for an up tick (increase) in the share price above the windows or a down tick (decrease) below the windows.

You wait patiently. You consult your "Dead Cat Bounce" manual. Give it three more weeks. If share prices slip lower, then you monitor the share price for another two weeks **at a minimum** before you commit any funds. You watch the market for more buying activity. You watch for an increase in the number of shares traded.

The decisions and choices are difficult. You wonder if you should you put all of your money in one company. You decide on a plan.

You divide your available funds by four. You buy two stocks. You invest one fourth of your funds in each one. At that point you still have one half of your funds in cash.

You continue to monitor the companies. If they drop lower, then you can buy again at the lower price. If the stocks move up, then you can buy more shares and feel good about the low prices paid.

The news media, the politicians, and the business TV programs are going berserk! They present a blend of good and bad news on the world's suffering economies. There is finger pointing and blame everywhere. Good news! The market is up slightly. Bad news! The market is down slightly. *Blah, blah, blah.* The market pays no attention to the news media. You continue to watch the share prices for an up tick and a volume increase.

You watch the Ten Most Active Stocks on the New York Stock Exchange (NYSE) and the Ten Most Active Stocks on the NASDAQ. The business section of the paper prints the Most Active Traded Stocks on the NYSE and the NASDAQ. These companies had the largest number of shares that traded yesterday.. These companies are **possibly** the most sought after by investors. You check the stocks to see which ones are holding up or advancing.

In your strategy room on your wall and in a three ring loose leaf binder you have a list of the "Top 25 **Internet** Stocks" and the "Favorite 25 **Companies** in America." You cut them out of the financial section in USA Today. There is another list of the "Top 25 **High Tech** Stocks" in the country from your local newspaper.

Texas Instruments (TXN) is one of the best liked companies in the "Top 25 High Tech Corporations." You like it. It is in the black and still turning a great profit every quarter. TXN is a well heeled manufacturer. It is also one of the top defense contractors. The shares are trading at $14 a share down from $37. This may be the low point. The shares are low enough to buy. You decide to spend twenty five percent of available funds on TXN. You go to your discount brokerage web site and arrange a buy order. With the simple click of a mouse the order is placed all of the way to the NYSE exchange trading floor.

You notice that CitiGroup traded **on thin ice** for one month at $3 a share. The NYSE floor brokers dropped it to $1. This is a whopping sixty six percent **decrease** from $3 to $1. CitiGroup was trading in the Ten Most Active and it fell to a $1 a share.

You laugh, "Ha! It serves them right!" Even kings of old and loan sharks from New England did not charge as much interest as CitiGroup. CitiGroup finally up ticked out of that window to a new window. Now, its share price is in a trading range fifty cents higher. A small positive upward rebound (up tick) is a good sign. You go to your discount broker's web page and place an order for $5,000 of CitiGroup. The second week it closes up at $1.75 per share. The next week it does not drop back down. In the third week it is over $2 and by the fourth week it is back at $3. CitiGroup is in 140 nations in the world. Buyers are scooping up Citi! The volume has picked up.

BANK OF AMERICA CORPORATION (BAC)

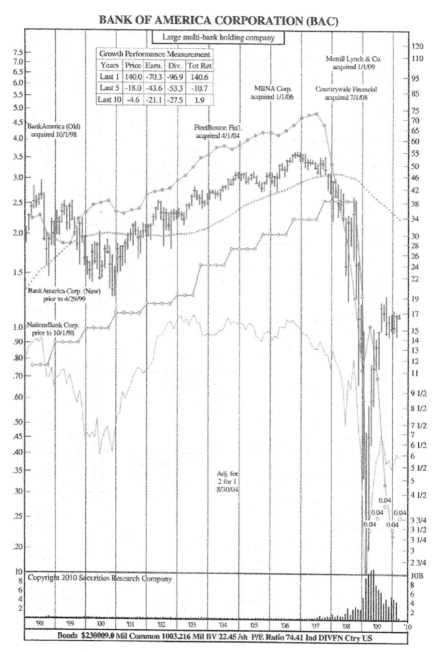

Chart provided by Securities Research Company
(SRC). Please visit www.srcstockcharts.com

CITIGROUP INC (C)

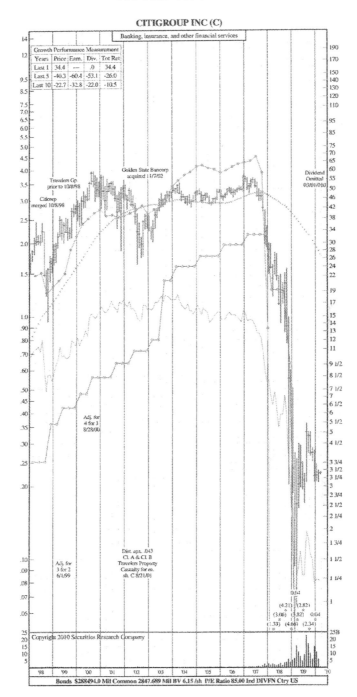

Chart provided by Securities Research Company (SRC). Please visit www.srcstockcharts.com

On the NYSE, Bank of America Corporation (BAC) has been trading in the top ten most active every day for two weeks at $3 a share. Somebody likes it! You consult the Securities Research Company chart book and note that just two years ago BAC was $50 in October of 2007. You look in the USA Today and BAC is listed in the "Twenty Five Most Popular" companies in the United States of America. How can this be? **The bank industry is in the tank!** These conflicting pieces of information are burning a hole in your head! You have personally suffered from the usurious rates those felons charge! **And that is why you buy it! You buy disaster!**

"The Devil!" you scream. It should be trading at $6.66!" This premonition compels you to immediately log on to the discount broker web page. You log in and place twenty five percent of your available funds into BAC. You buy 2,000 shares of Bank of America at $3 for a total cost of $6,000. **You buy disaster!** In a year or two BAC will be back up at $25. At $20 a share you would have $40,000! After taxes you would be able to pay down the home mortgage.

You ponder this thought and realize that you won! You caught the Dead Cat Bounce! You rise from your chair. Your arms and hands are in the air as you dance at the strategy table. **"Oh, yes! Me and the Devil!"** Your wife looks at you as if you are not the same man she married.

In less than twelve months, BAC recovered to $17.50 a share by August, 2009. $6,000.00 worth of BAC at $3 a share turned into $35,000.00 at $17.50 a share.

You missed Ford Motor Company. You snicker as you recall these terrible things you said during your younger years. "Found On Road in Ditch." "Fix Or Repair Daily." In July 2007, Ford shares traded at $7 down from $60. Ford has been as low as $2.50 in October, 2008. **The bargain basement fire sale share price was $1 to $1.65 in November, 2008.**

In less than twelve months, Ford recovered to $9 a share in December 2009. $5,000.00 worth of Ford (F) at $2 a share turned into $22,500.00 at $9 a share.

FORD MOTOR CO DEL (F)

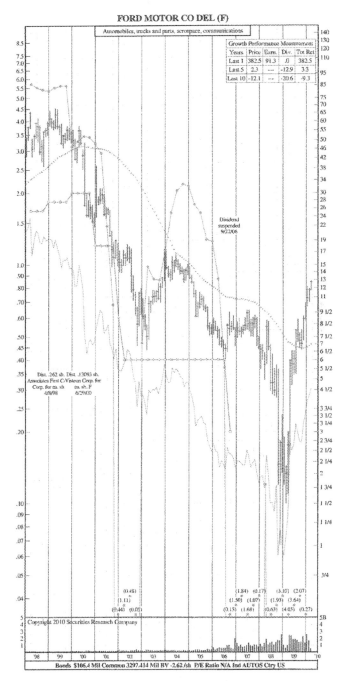

Chart provided by Securities Research Company
(SRC). Please visit www.srcstockcharts.com

Be careful! **You are on thin ice here.** Stocks have dropped from $20 or more per share down to $3 a share. There is still a problem at this price range. It is very easy for these shares to fall another fifty percent. CitiGroup was down to $3 for a couple of weeks. It **dropped another sixty six percent to $1.** It held at $1 for two weeks and began to move back towards $3. Ford had been at $5. Ford dropped to $2.50 and then to $1 in 60 days. **Ford dropped fifty percent two times in sixty days.** Be careful! Thin ice can break twice!

This is the Dead Cat Bounce environment. It is the pulse beat on a heart monitor. It is not a blip up every second. It is a straight horizontal line. The Dow Jones Industrial Average (DJIA) *is dead on the emergency room table* along with 2800 stocks on the NYSE and 3,100 on the NASDAQ. Share prices have dropped dramatically. The market is so oversold that share prices actually bounce up slightly. Thus the name, "Dead Cat Bounce."

The exchange floor traders are required by market rules to drop the price of stocks until buyers are found. This is the reason that stock prices will drop dramatically. (Sometimes referred to as a "free fall"). The free fall wipes out all of the good until cancelled orders and sell limit orders piled up on all of the desks and computers. No orderly price decline exists if there are no buyers. Prices drop like water going over Niagara Falls. If the shares have to fall to a dollar then it will happen.

The evil deed is done!

After the electrode paddles have been applied, the shares bounce up like a new blip on the heart monitor pulse line. The bargain hunters are back. Historically, they are a mixture of tightwads, mutual fund managers, greed mongers, treasure hunters and **all of them are astute bargain basement price shoppers.** After all, this is the easy way to make money.

New investors scamper in and take up the bargain buying opportunity. Others reel as they have been financially set back or destroyed. Some lose their entire savings, maybe even their livelihood. As you know, every dark storm has a cloud with a silver lining. Young adults can jump in and pursue their new livelihood. The elders had their chance but did nothing with it. The young look at the catastrophe and view it as the fault of the older generation. How could they let this happen?

This is it! This is **disaster** in the stock market! **This is the safest time to buy stocks!**

At this point we have to leave the Dead Cat Bounce scenario in order to discuss two important investment concepts, the four year business cycle and the greater fool theory.

THE 4 YEAR BUSINESS CYCLE

The goal of this book is to introduce new investors to the stock market. The language used is non technical so that concepts and theories can be easily understood. Most of the discussion in this book is based upon **an assumption that the business cycle is four years in length.**

Basically the cycle is a simple model of production output. Normally, the replacement of worn out goods and services is always occurring. If, however, there is an initial increase of a public demand for more goods and services, then production is stepped up for two years, in response to the increase until the demand has been met.

Once the new demand is met, then the level of production will taper off (over two years) and return to the original level of output. Simple. Two years up and two years down, a four year cycle.

In relation to an increase in production for two years, revenues and sales will go up for two years. Then, over years three and four, revenues and sales will level off and eventually return to their original level.

The share price of a company's stock is related to its revenues and sales, and the earnings/income that the company produces (measured in earnings per share of common stock, EPS). With an increase in revenue and sales, and EPS for two years, the share price of stock will increase. With a decrease in revenue and sales and EPS for two years, the share price of stock will decrease.

You may apply this cycle to the national economy. In other words, if there is an increase for goods and services, then over this cycle of four years the economy (the Gross National Product GNP includes foreign trades/imports and exports and the GDP, the Gross Domestic Product) and the stock market will expand in years one and two. Given that the demand for the additional increase has been met and that there is no further increase in demand, then the economy and stock market will contract in year three and four.

From 1965 to 1985 the DJIA index does mirror a four year cycle of two years up and two years down.

In the real world things are not that clear.

As the economy expands to a new level of production, it may hold that new level of production activity, if demand for additional goods and services remains. The economy may continue to expand further for another year or two, before demand for goods and services levels off or decreases.

The baby boom after World War II fueled a ten year economic expansion of goods and services.

If the financial market and economic expansion lasts for five or six years, then the sell off, or drop in the market is more sudden and more severe. The recession will last for a longer period of time than usual.

Occasionally, one industry may see continued expansion while other industries level off. The share price of companies in that industry will continue to rise if sales and revenue increase. The others will hold or decline.

The same is true for one particular company. If one company has an innovation or a new gizmo, then that company will grow when the new product is in great demand. It will outperform the competition.

If you own stock in one of these companies, you must remember that the share price will still drop in a market downturn. It will not drop as far as other companies as long as sales and revenues continue to outperform the competition. The share price is merely dragged down with the market slide (lack of buying activity), but it will rebound faster than the competitors.

Companies with good revenues and sales that turn out enormous volumes of product and merchandise or high dollar items in great demand will experience a thirty five to fifty percent drop in share price. Their revenues stay high because they are power houses. These kinds of companies are established household products, personal hygiene, health care, and pharmaceuticals. These shares recover fast and the momentum of the market may take these share prices higher than they were before the downturn.

Companies that do not have the leading product will feel a squeeze in sales and revenues. These companies may be down fifty to seventy percent in share price. They will be operating at a break even point. Their production and operation expenses will consume the sales and revenue income.

A few companies will not have any earnings during this period. They will be operating at a loss and surviving on income from last year.

Some shares drop seventy to ninety percent in price for no reason. They are not the favorites. No investors are interested in them. Fire sale shoppers are more interested in the popular companies.

Companies that are struggling to survive will drop seventy to ninety percent in share price. The size of the company is not a factor.

Massive cuts in consumer spending from coast to coast over a long recession will dry up sales and revenues. As a result some companies are forced to make drastic cost cutting measures (worker layoffs and plant closings) to keep operations intact.

These companies are flexible and they react rapidly to change so they can continue to operate and stay alive financially. Product output and operating profit may be fifty percent of what they were two years ago. The company will survive. They may make a profit on operations, but the company is only half in size of operations and profit of what it used to be. The share price may be slow to recover.

If the prospect of going out of business is imminent, then the share price might not experience a "Dead Cat Bounce." The share price would continue to drift lower. If the company manages to stay in business, the share price will be the last one to move up. It will be a poor performer, a dog. It may be the last stock out of approximately 6,000 to move up.

Do not confuse net income with operating and manufacturing income. Sales and revenues less (minus) operating and production expense results in operating income.

Net income is the very end result after the subtraction of administrative expenses and taxes payable from gross income. **In addition** the **current portion** (the partial amount due this month, quarter or year) of the **long term liabilities debt,** such as bond interest payable, bonds payable, dividends payable and bank loans payable (debts with a repayment schedule longer than five years) will all have to be subtracted form income. These current obligations may be so large that net income could actually be an enormous loss.

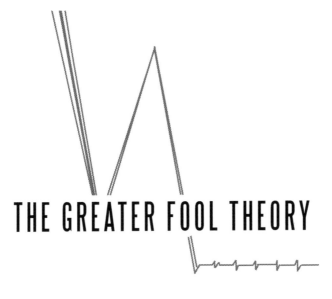

THE GREATER FOOL THEORY

Is the market a gamble? Yes it is! You better know what you are doing.

The Dead Cat Bounce makes assumptions and generalizations to facilitate learning.

The bottom triangle in the illustration represents all of the buyers and holders of the outstanding shares of one company from disaster day to the top price this share will reach in the next market peak.

As you near the $8 to $10 peak you invert the triangle. The upside down triangle on top represents all of the investors who want to sell at $8 to $10 dollars a share.

This illustration should remind you of the selling pressure that exists as share prices climb higher. Selling pressure is ever present. There is not enough room at the top for everyone to sell at $8 to $10 a share as there are **no more buyers left at this time**. The peak can not sustain all of these sellers, and the price will eventually drop back to $2 where everyone will become a buyer again.

This illustration is elementary; however, it has a large visual impact. The illustration is used to convey the idea that selling pressure exists and that it exists in a big way. Selling pressure is ever present. Are you a buyer or a seller? You are both!

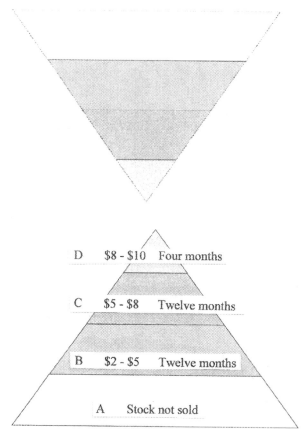

D	$8 - $10	Four months
C	$5 - $8	Twelve months
B	$2 - $5	Twelve months
A	Stock not sold	

Selling Pressure

Area A represents nine types of investor situations.

- **It represents those shares that were not sold in area D during the last market peak.**
- **It represents shares that are paid for and left in the market "to ride the tide."**
- It represents common or preferred shares of a corporation that have been contributed to IRA and Keogh retirement accounts.
- It represents inheritance and trust funds.

- It represents the shares of individual investors' mutual fund positions.
- It represents shares that are owned by other corporations and investors who for one reason or another have no desire to sell the stock.
- It represents positions required to be a major shareholder. One is required to own five percent or more shares of the company's outstanding stock in order to be a major shareholder.
- It represents stock that has been awarded to managers, executives, and CEOs.

Area B reflects the lowest share prices achieved in the last market disaster. It represents the **fire sale shoppers** and the bargain hunters. These are the first brave souls to jump into the bargain shopping fray of the disaster. Assume the share price is between $2 and $5 in Area B. This price range begins with the first month of the disaster and it lasts for twelve months. **It would be terrific if your IRA employer contribution is during Area B and not during Area D!**

Area C indicates the number of shares purchased between $5 and $8. The price range lasts for twelve months.

Area D indicates the number of shares purchased between $8 and $10. The price range lasts for four months. It has been two years since the fire sale disaster.

Assume you purchased shares in this company in Area B when the shares were selling for $2.50. You bought 5,000 shares at $2.50 for $12,500.00. You have held the shares for twelve months and the investment is worth $30,000 at $6 a share. You **hope** that the price might recover to $10. You consult your Dead Cat Bounce manual and review the four year business cycle. You wonder what direction the market is going and where it will be in the next twelve months. You play with the two triangles on your desk. You decide that the economy will begin to slow in the next four to six months and that you must sell your investment before the price begins to decline.

Everyone is happy. The economy has recovered and is humming along nicely. The media and the nightly business reporters are all smiles. Everything is grand. The Dow Jones continues to set record highs day after day by inching up one tenth of one percent. The neighbors are buying new things. The prices of gold and oil are beginning to decline. People are getting better jobs or promotions. You feel a false sense of overconfidence. You could sell 4000 shares now and leave 1000 shares to "ride the tide." You have held the shares for over a year and a half.

Four months later the stock is trading at $7.50. You are overjoyed. Your wife is begging you to sell. You decide to hold for another dollar or two. Rumor on the street is that the stock is on the way to $12 a share. Rumors are the same thing as lies. You wonder who would pay $7.50 a share. You realize they are first time buyers. They have finally saved enough money to buy a stock that has already doubled or almost tripled in price.

The stock has resistance and trouble moving above $8. You check into your strategy room. You read the Greater Fool Theory again. The Dead Cat Bounce manual points out that you are in the D Area of the triangle. You turn the second triangle upside down over the first. Woah! You realize the stock is not going to make it to $10. You discover that the short sales positions are very large.

Your wife gives you the ultimatum, "If you do not sell the stock, then I am going to divorce you." Woah! You check the financials on Yahoo Finance and discover that **the income this quarter is lower than income last quarter.** Gross revenues and sales are down.

The share price *has run out of greater fools*. The profits are shrinking. The buyers have walked away and the hype is no where to be heard. The company output has dropped. The trading volume is smaller than usual.

You call your discount broker and ask him to sell your shares immediately. He enters a sell order "at the market" which means that your shares will be sold **next** before any other seller, regardless of how long they have been waiting.

The sale is made at $7.82 per share. You receive $39,100.

You sold the stock! You recovered your original investment! What a wonderful profit. Your wife loves you madly. Once again you are the knight in shinning armor!

You bask in your tenacity and wisdom. You are euphoric and you want to make another trade and make some more money. You consult the Dead Cat Bounce manual and it reminds you that this specific time is a cooling off period. It will be at least two years before the next market disaster. Let the market go, but maintain an interest and continue to monitor favorite stocks. Pay down the home mortgage and the credit cards. Look for a desirable plot of land that will appreciate in price over ten years. Or, look for some inexpensive acreage outside of town to purchase. Use the time productively to broaden investor IQ and conduct productive research. The library business section and reference section will increase your knowledge and understanding of accounting, finance and economics. This will help you understand the financial statements. Some libraries have company annual reports.

Your wife spends the rest of the day reminding you that she has spent three years in a dreary kitchen that needs to be remodeled. The house needs to be painted. She tells you that the second hand furniture and car that you bought to save money are falling apart, and that you should quit playing the stock market while you are ahead. You just got lucky.

You remind your wife that you endure the dreariness as well. You emphasize that every cent of the profit is your money and that you will be the one to make the tough decisions. You decide to pay down the mortgage with $28,000. $11,000 remains in the brokerage account.

One month later the stock that you sold breaks out to the $8 range on a large increase in volume. You continue to monitor. Slowly the stock begins to move to $9. **Buyers under $7 were getting out!** At this time and later in the stage of the price decline you notice that an increase in the amount of short sales. The real market pros are "betting" that the price is going to drop even more. The price has been held up by short term trading activity. The short term investors have finally quit buying and they are waiting for the drop in the market and share prices before they become buyers again. The following month the stock holds at $9 on low volume. The price finally begins to decline. Three months later the stock is back under $7.50

Use this downtime to find some low price stocks of oil and gold producers. Compile a list of both. Buy a used computer and a monthly internet service provider. Go online. Pick up one to five shares of two low price oil producers and two low price gold producers. The graphs from Securities Research Company will show you the companies that exhibited some volatility in the last gold and oil run up. Monitor them in the online brokerage account portfolio as well as your five favorite companies.

Research gold and find out that ninety eight percent of the world's gold is still in the ground. You recall some of the hype that circulated with the gold speculation. "Gold is going to $3000 an ounce." You decide to make notes and start a folder on gold with a list of all the gold mining and exploration companies from $2 to $100 that trade on the NYSE and the NASDAQ exchanges. Some of the gold exploration companies that trade in the pink sheets do not have **proven reserves.** They only own leases or the mineral rights and are looking for or selling "limited partnerships." The leases and mineral acreage has yet to be fully explored.

Companies in the pink sheets that trade "Over the Counter" (with the help of the NASDAQ are typically very small and have no money for operations (under capitalized). Few of them are making money. Do not bother with the pink sheets or any "pink or penny stock" information/lies/rumors you receive in the junk mail to your home. Stay with the NASDAQ and NYSE exchange stocks.

Tidy up your strategy area. Make two photo copies of the two triangles. They remind you of the radioactive warning sign and the yellow caution sign. Keep one pair in your strategy folder in the desk drawer. The other pair goes on the strategy room wall next to the 100 year DJIA index wall chart from Securities Research Company. Next to the index chart is the 8.5 x 11 paper with your hand drawn graph that predicts when the market should begin to decline. You adjust it somewhat to the time that you believe the next fire sale shopping disaster day will occur. You are wise and you are monitoring the market for downward moves. You are waiting two years for the big price decreases in your five favorite stocks.

This is the phenomena of the Greater Fool Theory. Sell the stock by the time it moves into the D Area. When the share price gets into the D area, it may be two or three times higher than it was at the beginning of the base building in Area B during the last disaster. That is good enough. You are almost two years into the recovery. If the growth demand has been met, then production will slow. Based on a four year business cycle the next two years will be in decline until the demand for goods and services increases once again.

What actually happened from Area B to Area D? The share price is moving up and down, on its way in an orderly fashion to the price it traded during the last market peak. It is similar to an auction in as much as the bids start out very low and move progressively higher. **Everyone briefly owns the outstanding shares as the price moves up and down along the way from Area B to Area D.** The share price pattern may move back and forth between $3 and $5 in Area B two or three times before the share price pattern breaks out into Area C. Once in Area C, the share price pattern may move back and forth between $5 and $7 two or three times. Announcements every three months of quarterly gains in revenues and operating profits compared with the same quarter one year before will be one of the reasons for these fluctuations.

The share price pattern moves back and forth between the level of support (buyers) and the level of resistance (sellers). The share price may advance five to fifteen percent (from a support level) before selling is encountered at the new resistance level. This happens every quarter. It is due to the forthcoming announcement of the earnings report.

Short term investors take advantage of these price fluctuations. If the share price meets resistance (heavy selling, perhaps at the announcement of a poor quarterly performance), then the short term investor will sell and wait for the share price to fall back to the last level of support. Once the share price has dropped back to the previous support level the investor becomes a buyer again. It is possible that this type of opportunity will be present five or as many as eight times on the way from Area B to Area D.

Some investors buy once and **hope** to sell at a higher price. Some investors will make fifty percent one time and they will buy and sell only once. A few will make one hundred percent on the way up and they will buy and sell only once. They may hold the stock longer than one year which may give them a smaller tax to pay on the gain (Tax break for long term capital gains on stocks held for more than 12 months). Tax rules are changed periodically, so you will have to check current rates. The important point here is that the investors **made their gains on the way up and they got out on the way up.**

They did not wait until Area D. **They got out in Area C or just as the price moved into Area D.**

Short term investors are not concerned about taxes. They want only to make a profit. They do not want to risk holding a stock for a long period of time. **Short term investors do not want to lose one penny.** They are ruthless in this regard. They are willing to pay the tax on their total short term gains for the year. **They are not willing to lose money on a trade.** They watch the stock rise and take the five, ten or fifteen percent or more profit while the price is up. The short term investor knows that a share price can pass through the resistance level and go higher **only if there is a steady stream of buyers and continued reports of good news** on the company.

By tax law, corporations report only twenty percent of their short term trading profits as part of their short term income. This is not a heavy tax and this is one reason that institutions participate in an enormous amount of short term trading.

A mutual fund does not pay taxes on its trades. The taxes are and paid by the individual who sells the shares, unless the shares are sheltered in a tax free vehicle such as an IRA. This allows the mutual fund companies to participate in an enormous amount of short term trading.

MANIAS

There is another possible outcome for Area D. This is something to keep in mind. Area D can be a "Mania" area. A **mania** will allow share prices to climb over and above the share price peak in the previous market cycle. Share prices can increase five or ten times more than the original purchase price. $1,000 can become $10,000.

You could possibly see twenty times your money. If you recognize that a gizmo or new product will take the industry by storm in the next five years, then you could see $1000 turn into $20,000 or $10,000 turn into $200,000.

A Mania can be associated with a craze or a fad. It could be the gold craze. It could be the oil jihad craze.

A mania could be a new product or invention that opens up a whole new industry. It could be a new product that outperforms old products in an existing industry.

New products or replacement products that perform better than the old standard will eventually find acceptance. It could be a product that adds greater efficiency to the office, the production process, the construction area, the transportation area or to the home.

It could be a new resource or product that competes with or eventually replaces an old commodity. Computers and new software technology raised employee efficiency and company output. Cell phones and the internet provide instant communication. These companies have enjoyed real surges in their stock price as they announced new products.

Sometimes a mania is within just one industry or just one company. A company that brings a new product to the public that is in high demand will experience growth in sales and revenue along with a corresponding increase in stock price, perhaps for several years.

An announcement of FDA approval on a miracle drug or a miracle medical cure will send a stock price soaring. Announcements of a cure for cancer in the 1940's sent a particular stock soaring. Searle (USA), Schering (Germany), Syntex (Great Britian), marketed the enovid birth control pill in the 60's. They enjoyed magnificent gains in stock price.

On occasion a mania will take the form of a large national consumer movement. Remember the Dot Com Boom? The new generation was in. The old was on its way out. The Dot Com Boom brought the world together through the internet. The Dot Com Boom brought a new generation of investors to the stock market. They were young and savvy. The world was theirs! ***The internet was going to save the world!***

A number of Dot Com companies saw share prices increase by twenty times. Many investors increased their wealth. They may not have become millionaires, but they certainly made their lives much easier financially as they became debt free! Some investors made small fortunes. Some increased their wealth to over a million.

The upward move in share prices began in 1998. The NASDAQ Composite Index moved from 1500 in 1998 to a whopping 4200 **in just two years. For nine months the NASDAQ Composite Index remained between 3600 and 4200** (almost one year). This broad, long lasting spike is very impressive. There was one narrow spike to 5000 over a fifteen day period during this time.

In October of 2000, the NASDAQ began to decline. The trading volumes were phenomenal. Compare the volume in 1998 and 1999 to the volume during the downturn years 2000 and 2001.

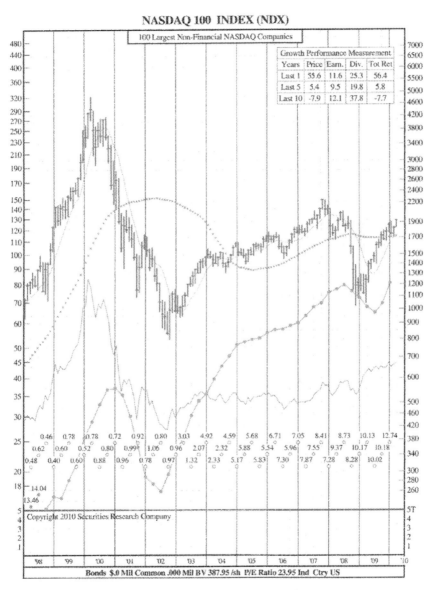

Chart provided by Securities Research Company (SRC). Please visit www.srcstockcharts.com

These new companies began modestly in the nineties. The companies required annual membership or purchase of software. Every year they gained more subscribers and online advertising revenue.

Every year new memberships and more revenue from sales and advertising kept revenues increasing in large percentages compared to the previous year. The internet may have been a little slow at the time, but there was everything to like and nothing to dislike.

Everyone heard the story. The stocks become favored by investors. Netscape. AOL. Yahoo. Ebay. Microsoft. Amazon. Everyone climbed on board. Everyone saved up some cash to invest in stocks with membership growth that became staggering to the imagination. The rest is history.

Existing companies related to the computer industry participated in the run up (Apple).

APPLE INC (AAPL)

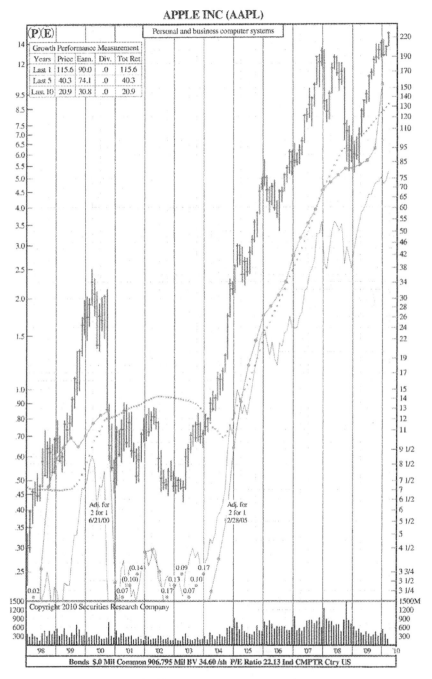

Chart provided by Securities Research Company
(SRC). Please visit www.srcstockcharts.com

AMAZON COM INC (AMZN)

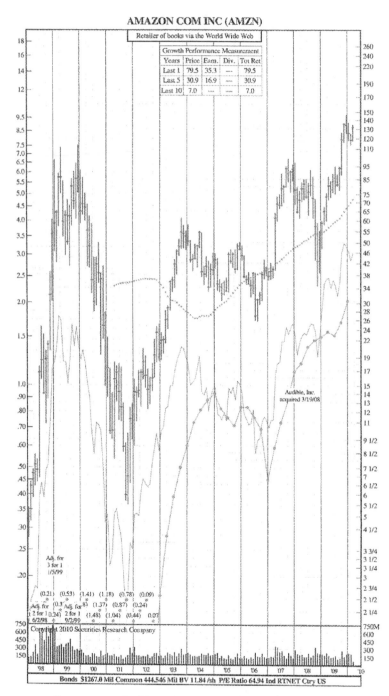

Retailer of books via the World Wide Web

Growth Performance Measurement				
Years	Price	Earn.	Div.	Tot Ret
Last 1	79.5	35.3	---	79.5
Last 5	30.9	16.9	---	30.9
Last 10	7.0	---	---	7.0

Audible, Inc.
acquired 3/19/08

Adj. for
3 for 1
1/5/99

(0.21) (0.53) (1.41) (1.18) (0.78) (0.09)
Adj. for (0.3) Adj. for (1.37) (0.87) (0.24)
2 for 1 0.24) 2 for 1 (1.48) (1.04) (0.44) 0.07
6/2/98 9/2/99

Copyright 2010 Securities Research Company

Bonds $1267.0 Mil Common 444,546 Mil BV 11.84 /sh P/E Ratio 64.94 Ind RTNET Ctry US

Chart provided by Securities Research Company
(SRC). Please visit www.srcstockcharts.com

Look at the chart for Amazon. On the bottom horizontal axis is the trading volume and a unit of time. Each vertical line represents all of the shares traded during one month. The number of all of the shares traded is noted and "read" on the scale of measurement at the very bottom right hand corner (150 million to 750 million) of the vertical axis.

The vertical axis on the right also indicates the share price (2.25 to 260).

The Amazon rise was like a rocket. In January of 1998 it was trading at just above $4 a share. In six months it met resistance in the $18 area. It traded in the $18 area for five months. A large volume of shares changed hands. In November, it broke out to the $30 range. In December it was in the $50 range. The following year Amazon was in the $65 range with an occasional leap over $85.

In January of 2000, Amazon began its decline. It returned to the $5 to $7 fire sale area for three months at the end of 2001.

If you are so fortunate to have stock trading in a mania, then you need to adjust the selling strategy. At some point you need to recover the original investment. Would you sell thirty five percent of your shares if the stock doubled or tripled in price? The other sixty five percent could be left in the market to "ride the tide?" This decision is left up to you. It is easy with hindsight.

Hopefully, every reader of the Dead Cat Bounce will be a participant in a mania someday, and have to make such wonderful decisions.

WHAT YOU NEED TO KNOW: THE MISSOURI PACIFIC RAILROAD BONDS

One beautiful summer afternoon an account executive (stockbroker) was phone canvassing (bothering people at home or work) in search of potential investors. The broker was using phone numbers obtained from a book of street listings at the library. He was "dialing for dollars." One phone call connected to a man in a wealthy neighborhood. Quite by accident a pleasant conversation began. Politely, not to be out of line, the broker asked the gentleman how he found his riches.

Here is the answer. Brace yourself.

"It was the Monday following December 7, 1941 (the Japanese attack on Pearl Harbor). The Missouri Pacific Railroad Bonds ($1,000 face value for each bond) opened for trading at $1.00 a bond. I was thirty years old. I was just out of college. I had majored in finance. I sold everything I had but my toothbrush. I was able to acquire 1500 Missouri Pacific bonds. I had to wait awhile before they recovered. It was several years, but I hung on to them."

This young man knew he could increase his wealth without risk. When World War II began the news sent the stock market tumbling down. Disaster was at the door step. The young man did not hesitate. Disaster was everywhere and he jumped in with every dollar he could find.

What does this tell you? Can an investor strike it rich in the stock market?

By now you know that the answer is, **"Yes!"** You will win here before you ever win the lotto. The stock market could change your life. Participate even if you begin on a small level. Get started and become familiar with this environment. Discover that **you really can win**. There is much to learn. The key is to be ready.

Find a discount broker website that you like and open a free account. It can all be done online over the internet. Have the social security and the driver license numbers handy. Mail a deposit or arrange for a wire transfer of funds between your bank and the brokerage house. Not on the net? Go to 1 800 555 1212 (toll free) phone information and ask for the 800 phone number of the discount broker.

It could be the best move you ever make.

Do not spend much money. Buy five shares of a couple of stocks. As a hobby read the news on the Ten Most Active stocks, and the Ten Most Declined stocks. Follow trends. Follow up ticks and down ticks. Continue to learn. Educate yourself.

There are new brokers every month beginning a career in the securities industry. Almost every state gives a state regulatory test for the NASD (National Association of Securities Dealers) Series Seven exam in order to be licensed and registered in the state to sell securities as a registered representative (stockbroker) for a brokerage house or as an insurance agent. If the candidates are smart, they will pay for both the insurance license and the stockbroker license. Insurance sales is better for the long haul. A career as a stockbroker is usually less than a year unless you are working for a discount broker on a salary rather than a sales commission.

The cram course for a Series Seven Securities License is one week. Your internet search engine (Yahoo or Google, etc.) will give you all the information if you search "NASD Series Seven Exam." The candidates come from all walks of life. The average age is twenty nine. Some might have a bit of knowledge of the market, but for the most part these future brokers will learn the market the hard way.

This is a self help discipline. Education will get you a job. **You have to find wealth by yourself.** This will require persistence and desire, but you already have an edge over the new brokers. You have the Dead Cat Bounce.

There is one more book to buy to "Seal the deal." This book is mandatory for your success. It is the Orange Book from Securities Research Company.

Visit www.srcstockcharts.com on the internet. You must visit this web site. Check to ensure that indeed you are on the **Securities Research Company** web site. Their logo is "Trusted by Investors since 1933."

Click on "Chart Books." Select the Orange Book. The Orange Book consists of 1500 charts of the **most actively traded** stocks on the NASDAQ exchange.

These charts will visually enhance your perception and knowledge of the effect that a major market correction will have on the share prices of company stocks.

The charts from Securities Research Company clearly illustrate

- The dramatic drop of the share price of a stock during a severe market downturn.

- The length of time that a stock remains at the lowest price.

- The length of the base building period before a stock resumes an upward move.

- The number of shares (volume) that trade every month.

- The areas of resistance where selling (profit taking) is encountered.

The charts will confirm the concept *that a steep stock market decline is the safest time to buy shares of stock.*

These charts will help you associate the main premise of this book with your fire sale shopping habits. "Buy low and sell high" is not the main premise. **The main premise of the Dead Cat Bounce is to** *"Buy Disaster."*

The Orange Book and the Blue Book allow you to compare the day of disaster of many different companies and industries to one another.

You will begin to realize that not all 6,000 stocks can have their low point on the same day at the same time. Over the six to nine month bottom of the market, not all 6,000 stocks will have their low point on the very day that the DJIA index hit its lowest point. Some industries lead the way and are the first to suffer. Some well healed companies that still pump out the product and collect the revenue will only drop thirty five to forty percent and recover within a month or two. Some companies bottom out after all of the others have begun to move up.

Trust me. The Orange Book is vital to your success.

Do not flinch. Do not hesitate. The cost of the book is $100. For $25 more you can have the book and a three month online membership that allows you to download daily updates on many stocks that trade on the NASDAQ. The Securities Research Company website will provide you with knowledge and valuable technical advice.

In this book you may find a stock that will continually increase in price or a dynamic company that will continually outperform the competition. You might find one stock that you can trade over and over for the rest of your life once you learn and understand its pattern.

MARKET DOWNTURNS

Thirty corporations make up the Dow Jones Industrial Average index. The companies have been changed at times to get rid of old dogs. Vibrant performers are required. After all, the movement of the index must reflect the direction that the 2800 companies are moving toward.

On the very bottom horizontal scale of the DJIA Index chart, each **year** has twelve vertical lines.

Each line represents the time element of one month. The length of the line represents the total number of shares traded in the thirty companies of the index. The length of the line (volume) is measured with the small scale on the bottom right corner. The scale measurements read 100 million through **500 million** for the DJIA Index chart for years 1982 to 1993. For the DJIA Index chart with the years 1998 through 2009, the scale measurements read 3 billion through **15 billion.**

The vertical scale on the right side of the graph represents the index value. When the index value is graphed, the index path reflects (hopefully) **the direction of the share price path of the 2800 stocks that trade on the NYSE.**

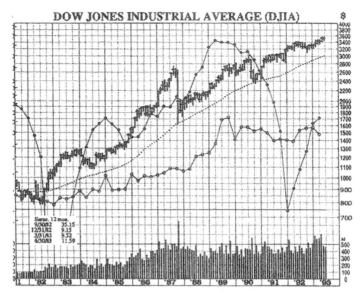

Chart provided by Securities Research Company
(SRC). Please visit www.srcstockcharts.com

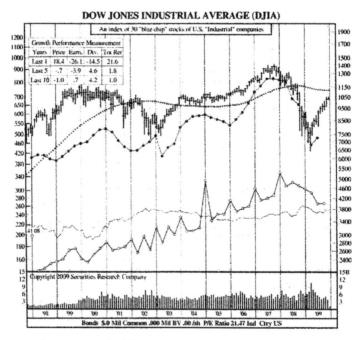

Chart provided by Securities Research Company
(SRC). Please visit www.srcstockcharts.com

In 1980 and 1981 the NYSE exchange volume for approximately 2800 stocks was normally 20 million shares for an average day. 10 million shares traded on a slow day, and active, heavy days were 40 million shares. There were two exceptions to this. Two enormous trading days occurred with the steep decline of the downturn in January, 1980 and August of 1981. The name given to this event is "panic selling." The phone lines at the brokerage firms were jammed. Not all investors could reach their brokers in time to sell their stock positions. The volume surged on these days to 86 million and 94 million.

In 1988, 188 million shares was the average number of shares traded each day. 600 million was traded on the few big days and 80 million traded on the slow days.

The year 2000 saw the first trading days of over 1 billion shares.

Find the year 1987. Two years of mania trading and investing (1986 and 1987) were required to build and move the DJIA index from 1600 up to 2600. In October, 1987, the DJIA index fell from approximately 2600 to almost 1650 in thirty days. Talk about disaster!

In November, the index range jumped up 200-400 points to a range between 1800 and 2000. The low point in December was back down to about 1750. Note the length of the December line. For the thirty days of December, 1987 the DJIA **index** range was between 1750 to 2000.

This "rebuilding phase" or "consolidation phase" usually lasts six months **with regard to the DJIA index**. The actual recession will be longer than a year.

The drop in October, 1987 wiped out the 1000 point index **gain made in two years of mania trading** and investing in 1986 and 1987. It was **two years after the crash** before the DJIA index made it back to the 2600 high of 1987. This is consistent with all market downturns.

During this precipitous decline the market dropped over three hundred points on two days. One day was actually over 400 points.

The largest trading volumes were a couple of days with well over 100 million shares. This might lead one to pose the question, "Does the market drop like a rock off a cliff?" The answer is, "**You bet it does!**"

Shortly after the steep decline in October, 1987, the Securities Exchange Commission quickly passed a new exchange trading regulation. The law stated that after a drop of two hundred points the trading exchange would be shut down for the day. The law would **hopefully** provide time for the panic selling frenzy to cool off.

Compare the monthly trading volume in 1980 and 1981 to 1986 and 1987.

How did the volume of the number of shares increase so dramatically?

Several phenomena are responsible for the increase in the number of shares traded on a day to day basis between these periods of time.

- Computer software trading programs on the home computer and the internet link investors and institutions to the security dealers' floor brokers. Trades can be placed instantly by comparison to the out dated telephone line services. The middle 80's saw the rise of discount brokerage companies. The 90's saw the increase in home computers. Securities companies began to issue software that would allow investors to follow the market and enter trades over the internet right from their homes.

- Corporations have authorized and issued large amounts of common stock that have been used to acquire capital (plant, equipment, and machinery) or to purchase or to merge with another company. In 1980, Exxon Corporation had **500 million** shares of outstanding stock. This was the largest amount of any American company. Today, Exxon has over

1.5 billion shares of common stock outstanding. Currently, many companies on the NYSE and NASDAQ exchanges have billions of shares of common stock outstanding (issued by the companies to the public). CitiGroup now has **26 billion shares after the bailout.**

- Corporations increased their reserves of common stock authorized and issued the common shares for employee retirement accounts to provide their employees access to shares for contributions to their retirement funds.

- The number of short term investors and the volume of short term trades increased dramatically. Shares now trade in millionths of a second.

- The number of international investors and businesses and the amount of trading they do has increased.

- Mutual funds and brokerage houses participate in short term trading for their investors and for their own benefit as well. Both have access to enormous amounts of money.

Here is a recent example of short term trading.

Huntington Bancshares had less than 500 million shares outstanding before the market crash. Now 716 million shares are outstanding for public trading. Between January, 2009 and February, 2010, over **6 billion** shares have traded in the market. This is six times greater than the 716 million shares. Truly, this is a phenomenal amount of short term trading.

Short term trading has always existed in the market. Today it exists in a big way.

The stock markets consist of an enormous number of **short term investors.** These investors have one goal. That goal is to buy stocks that are moving up and sell as the stock meets resistance. Short term investors buy and sell shares within two weeks, a week, a few days, or a few hours. They are not interested in holding a stock position longer than twelve months (long term investors) just to save a few dollars on any IRS tax break given to a long term gain (holding a stock for more than twelve months before selling). That would be a loss of valuable opportunities.

Short term traders play resistance levels.

Share prices rise to a resistance level where they encounter enough selling to knock the share price down five percent. Buying resumes and another upward move to the resistance level is encountered once again.

Sometimes a resistance level will have a trading range of five percent of the share price. If the resistance level and the trading range last for one month on an actively trading company stock, then one or two trades for four percent or more can be made. If you can do this ten months in a row, then you may be an expert short term trader.

Short term investors play disaster scenarios.

When a company has bad news the stock price will drop. As long as the company is healthy and still producing a **profit from operations** the share price will recover. The most recent example is British Petroleum (BP). BP fell from $60 on the news of the Gulf oil spill. BP shares began to build a new base at $30 and have moved up towards $40.

For short term investors the market is not to **buy and hope or hold a stock for the long term.** This would be the mind set of a loser. The market exists to buy and win!

HUNTINGTON BANCSHARES INC (HBAN)

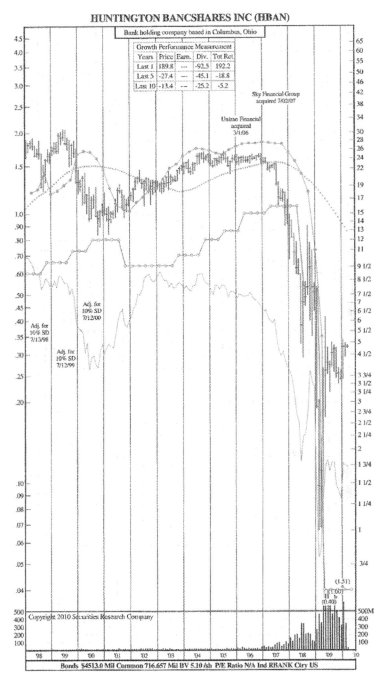

Chart provided by Securities Research Company
(SRC). Please visit www.srcstockcharts.com

Return to the DJIA index chart and the years from 1982 through 1987. Ask yourself what events led up to this dramatic rise in the average. This expansion was due to a mania. It was not a mania in the sense that the Dot Com Boom was a mania. This expansion was a result of a strong belief that the market would rise.

During the stagflation years after the Viet Nam War the market was trading in a narrow range in the late 70's and early 80's. It was an opinion of many prominent brokerage firms (security dealers) that the market had lacked participation from investors in years past and that share prices did not reflect the true value of prospering companies.

Wall Street and the financial communities from coast to coast **touted** that the DJIA index **was on its way to 3000!** Perhaps this was optimistic, but after all, the market had been held back in the 70's and early 80's. A good announcement (rumor) was needed to get the market back into action. The sentiment on the street was that share prices would climb and the DJIA index would soon be on the way to 3000.

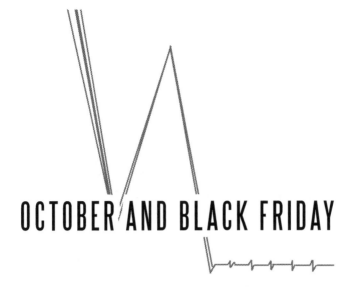

OCTOBER AND BLACK FRIDAY

It takes a long time to close the books at the end of a year. **The end of the fourth business quarter and the business calendar year end is June 30.** This is a good time to close out the end of the year financial statements as there are no back to back holidays (Thanksgiving, Christmas, and New Years) to interrupt this extensive project. There is barely enough time at the end of the civilian calendar year (your normal civilian year end December 30) to get the 1099s and the W2s printed up for the employees.

At the end of the year, after the financial statements have been prepared and completed, the statements must be approved and closed for the year by the BOD (Board of Directors).

A company audit is performed by an independent group of auditors.

The auditors review the company records. They affirm that the financial statements are ninety eight percent accurate. Blah, blah, blah.

Summation of the data for the entire year is compared to the year end data of the previous two to four years in the annual report for the shareholders and potential investors. Hopefully, this comparison reflects a pattern of increased sales and earnings.

The first fiscal (business) quarter of the **corporate year** is July, August and September. It ends September 30. When September 30 passes the results of the **first** quarter financial statements are completed.

It may seem as if nothing is going on in the markets during August and September. Everyone has forgotten about the stock market. Parents are getting ready to get the kids back to school. Everyone is saving their money for the upcoming holidays, Thanksgiving and Christmas. It appears no one really cares what is going on in the markets.

Folks, you can bet your waders that the serious short term investors are trying to find out the results of the first quarter reports. Make no mistake. The decision to sell or "lighten up" is being made at this juncture.

After all, December will be a heavy selling month for stocks that have not produced a gain in order for the investor to be eligible to receive a short term loss deduction on his IRS income tax return. Stocks are slow to move upward in December due to the holidays and the sales for the short term loss IRS tax deduction, not to mention any short sales that may have been placed in October by the pros and risk takers who bet that the market was going to drop.

The thrust of all the concern is this.

Is the company moving ahead in sales, revenues and income? Is it ahead of the previous quarter and is it ahead of the previous quarter a year ago? Is it ahead of the competition?

This news will in fact have an effect on which way the share price will move.

Investors are chomping at the bit. Good news and good news only keeps stocks poised at their current price. Bad news will send stocks lower temporarily.

The reports must reflect at minimum that the company is holding steady or advancing with regard to profit and production. Anything less than that will culminate in a five percent or greater decline of the share price, as these announcements become public. This news is often "leaked" and shares will begin to decrease in value fifteen to thirty days before the announcement is to be made. You can bet an eraser all of the chief operating officers of every department will lose their skin if this year is not better than last.

If the company growth and the economy are in the doldrums, then the company may be losing profit and production may be shrinking. If the year is down and the first quarter is down at the end of September 30, then the short term investors will not do anymore buying. They will check the earnings reports of companies in the same industry to determine if an industry wide slowdown exists. If there is not an industry wide slowdown, then the active investors will look for shares in companies that are reporting better revenues and earnings.

Investors will wait to see if the effect is small or large on the common share price. If the price backs off a bit but holds, then investors and short term investors become buyers. If the price continues to drop, then this will precipitate more selling. The share prices will slide as much as ten to fifteen percent.

October is the month where all of this innuendo is taking place and the market reacts accordingly to the **facts, lies, and rumors** of the time. If the news is bad, then October reacts with short term buyers turning into sellers. If the news is good, then short term investors buy shares moving up. If the market stays healthy, then the market may advance through the second quarter and the Thanksgiving and Christmas holidays.

October is often a rough month because of this scrutiny. If buyers and sellers draw the conclusion that prices are in a downtrend by the end of the first fiscal/business quarter, September 30, then the share price drop occurs in October. If the entire economy and market is in a downturn, then Black Friday appears!

Are you a buyer or a seller? You are both. It would be great to buy and have the share go up forever, but it does not always work that way. We have to be buyers and sellers based upon what we see happening and what we know from the past.

THIN ICE

The Dead Cat Bounce makes assumptions and generalizations in order to facilitate learning. The next three pages will be repetitious in order to communicate the phenomena and the intricacies of the **"fire sale environment."** Professional analysts, chartists and other associated disciplines may not be in agreement with the descriptions or the terminology. Please be tolerant. The reader will find correct terminology as time goes on.

When you are **fire sale shopping** while walking on thin ice it is necessary to watch the number of shares traded (volume) and the share price movement. Keep a record so you can compare the volumes and the stock price moves to the previous days and weeks. Use the **"window"** to chart the path.

A share price will fluctuate during the trading day. It may go up or down a few cents to the next trade. The share price will fluctuate up and down in a normal range of one to two percent of the total share price. Sometimes the range is two to four percent. We are going to refer to this range as the **"window."**

For example a $10 dollar stock will fluctuate during the trading day in a small range of (say arbitrarily) twenty five to thirty five cents. It is usually trading at $10 but one day it might be down thirty five cents and the next day it might be up thirty five cents.

Track this window. A path will appear that will indicate if the share price is advancing or declining. In fire sale disaster shopping, track the stocks to the lowest share price. At that point you have to determine if the price is holding and building a base from which the share price can move up without encountering (sellers) profit taking.

When you track a share price to the bottom of the crash it is best to use graphs that have the volume of shares **expressed in weeks or days** on the horizontal axis. This is easily done on the discount broker websites and Yahoo Finance. They have graphs of one trading day and five trading days. Print the graphs of the week out so you can review the trading price window and volume every day of the week. Keep the weeks in order. Now you have the price pattern every day in a row for a month.

If the price down ticks on **more volume**, small volume or no volume, then you are on *thin ice* and the price will go lower.

If the share price path has remained in the same area on small volume, large volume or no volume, then the shares may have built a base support level. The shares may be at the lowest price the share will experience.

With more up ticks than downticks on little volume, no volume or more volume, then the share price path will be moving up from this base building (support level) in a convincing manner.

Here is a pattern you need to remember. **The price moves up on little or no volume.** This is a good sign that there is demand for the stock. This is what to look for. **Determine that the large selling has finished.**

To be a winner, buy shares that are moving up.

You are going to be a winner.

Up ticks on little volume, occasionally, **indicate a forthcoming announcement of good news.** This is also an indication that buyers have returned and are willing to risk at this time. They are betting that the price path is going to go up and they are willing to pay the higher share price.

Quite often the word is out that quarterly earnings will be even with or a little bit ahead of last quarter. Typically, the price will have moved up five percent before the announcement. At the time of the actual announcement in the news, there will be heavy volume. This will be the short term investor profit taking/selling "on good news." The share price might rise another two or three percent, but that will be the high. The share price will slip back down to the price it was before it began to climb on the rumors of the good quarterly earnings.

Perhaps the rumor is that the earnings will exceed expectations. In this case the stock may advance a little more than five percent. After the official news announcement it may rise another two to five percent, again on heavy volume. The outcome will be the same. The short term investors will take their profits and the stock price will return to the price level before the rumors began. This effect will begin fifteen to thirty days prior to the end of every quarter.

Buyers of the shares on the official announcement of the "good news" will experience a five percent decline in the share price simply because they were buying two weeks too late. The stock price will fall back five percent after the official news announcement and the trading frenzy is over.

Caution is needed in the thin ice phase.

You could lose fifty percent of your money very quickly. The bottom of the market is not a bad time to have a gamble reverse, but remember that *the ice can break twice.* There are very often two drops in share price of fifty percent or more as a stock closes in on the low point.

The message here is to be on the safe side the first time you go fire sale shopping! The entire market is very close to the low point. Watch for the first 50 percent drop in stock prices.

Be patient and wait for the base building support phase. The window may still fluctuate a little higher or a little lower on small volumes. And there should be **no more declines other than a few small down ticks**.

Wait to make certain the price holds and that it holds on volume increases with an up tick.

Most **conservative fire sale shoppers** wait four weeks to be on the safe side.

The shortest waiting period to determine that a stock has bottomed out and that it has gained support is two weeks. To buy immediately after two weeks of no further decline is tempting and it can pay off with a larger return; however, you will be at risk. You will be taking more risk than you need to.

It is impossible to know this will be the lowest share price. If you buy, then please **commit only one fourth of your funds or less.** Should the stock drop another fifty percent from $3 to $1.50 or $1 to fifty cents place another one fourth of the funds at the new low price. The best thing to do is wait for the third week or at least until Thursday of the third week. If the stock jumps, up a quarter or fifty cents, then that is the sign to commit. Go for it.

Citigroup (C) was at a dollar for less than two weeks. If you jumped into the fire and bought it at $1 in the first week that the ice broke, when the price fell from $3 to $1, then you would double your gambling money. If you were watching but did not buy at $1 then you could have bought at $1.50 or $2 as it moved back to $3. A fifty percent return on a gamble in that very short period of time is **excellent!** This is the goal!

You win whether 1000 or 10,000 shares are purchased! Be proud. Never feel defeated or frustrated. Never feel disappointed that investing in a stock is useless or not enough of a gain. Be gratified that your selection and timing is correct.

What matters here is that you develop new skills that can be used again. Develop the skill to track share prices to the low point. Respect the interim period to ensure that the share price path is up. Develop the judgment for the correct time to purchase shares. This is a major accomplishment. Be proud of this accomplishment and pursue this endeavor with enthusiasm. **You will discover that you can change your financial life.**

The consolidation or rebuilding phase for the thirty companies that comprise the DJIA is approximately six months. The actual recession will last a year or more. As you go through this six to nine month phase of bottom fishing take notes. The unemployment figures will be dismal. The payrolls will continue to shrink. Mortgages will continue to see an increase in the number of foreclosures. Record these "economic and financial" thoughts that appear in the financial news. Print the graphs of the stocks you follow along with any good advice you find in other reputable sources. This will be valuable reference material for your next four ice walks.

In disaster fire sale shopping it is possible to buy and sell with fifty to one hundred percent profits more than once. After you have been through one down turn and witnessed the phenomena, you might be able to get two excellent trades the next time.

You will be surprised at how many times that you can make more than one good trade.

Okay. If you find the bottom of the market and possibly the low point of your favorite stock, this does not mean that you can kick back and grab the channel changer, or take off on a vacation. The base building phase is what the fire sale shoppers are watching for. A stock moving up from $1.25 to $2 will move to $3 much faster. This is a sure sign the buyers are back. If you have the channel changer in your hand you will miss the opportunity to buy the stock at the low point.

Often there will be a sudden **reverse in market direction**. This reverse is known as the **"double dip"** recession. There may be three to six months of **solid market base building** (at the markets low point). There may be a somewhat convincing broad market share price move from this consolidation that will last for three to four months possibly even a year.

However, if the recovery dries up and falters, **then the market will weaken and fall back.** If earnings reports are losing ground and the market begins to weaken and decline, then sell your positions.

As a stock moves to a higher level, make certain that the selling resistance/profit taking encountered remains small. Down ticks in share price must be small and they may occur occasionally, but downticks should not be linked day after day. They should be interspersed with up ticks and there should be a greater number of up ticks than downticks.

SELECTION

The environment and atmosphere that has been described in the last sixty pages is **the bottom of a severe stock market decline.** The parameters have been outlined. The assumptions and concepts have been presented to you.

By now you know that **the heart of disaster** is much different than the usual advice of "Buy low and sell high."

Disaster is the lack of a heartbeat in the emergency room. The market must be revived. Disaster begs the application of the defibrillator paddles because there are no more buyers. Disaster begs that share prices be dropped in order to find a price where buyers and sellers will begin to trade.

This method of **investing in disaster** has been used successfully by many investors over the last seventy years. Of all the strategies to make a profit in the market, investing in disaster happens to be the best. **It is not fool proof**. The correct time and the correct company selection is what will determine your success. *The author can not be held liable for bad selection or bad timing on the part of the reader.*

Now it is time to put a little perspective on **the selection of a good company**.

A good investor can diagnose a company by running some tests on financial statements.

The current assets ratio, the current liabilities ratio, the inventory ratio, operating margins, fixed ratio, and the working capital ratio will tell an investor if the company is performing poorly **due to inefficient operation**, or if the company is losing market share because the competition has a better product. The ratios are simple math.

Analysis will reveal if the company is an ongoing concern or if it is just a matter of a few months before the company has to close its doors.

At first it may seem that you are overwhelmed with detail, but with just a little bit of skull sweat you will be ready for the emergency room on disaster day. You will pick out the good companies and leave the bad ones alone. The bad ones will be the last to recover. It will take them longer than six months and any price increase will be small.

Here is an example.

Let's say you are **fire sale shopping** in the *disaster* environment. You have been watching several robust company stocks that are down forty to fifty percent from their highs of last year. They are your favorite choices.

The share price of one company not on your watch list has fallen eighty percent! Wow! You could make a bundle if that baby recovers in a year. The stock is under $5.

If the company is in financial trouble **it may get a small Dead Cat Bounce,** but afterwards the share price will continue to drift lower. **The ice will keep breaking** time and time again as the company may be headed out of business or into bankruptcy. **You will lose your hard earned money.** Even if the company emerges from bankruptcy there is no guarantee that it will be an ongoing concern (continue to operate as a business) or that the stock price will recover.

For instance, CitiGroup would have gone into bankruptcy at one dollar a share or less **if the government had not bailed them out.** The shares would have been suspended from trading on the exchange. In this instance if you play a hunch and purchase CitiGroup at $3 or $1 a share, then you may have money tied up in a bankruptcy for a year or more. If the company goes out of business, then you will lose your **hard earned dollars** due to a worthless stock selection. **You will miss other opportunities**. Most investors were keenly aware that the Federal Government would bailout the banking industry. This reduced the risk of purchasing the shares of CitiGroup.

In a similar example, Chrysler went into bankruptcy in 1979. The stock was trading at $1.25 a share. The bankruptcy court took control. The stock was suspended from trading by the Security Exchange Commission. A year later, Chrysler emerged from bankruptcy. The stock opened around $2.00 a share. It traded for 4 to 6 months between $2.50 and $5. It recovered to $15 a share within two years. The government bailout of American Motors Corporation in the 50's was very similar to Chrysler's situation.

A troubled company will not see an upward share price move. When it finally moves, it will be the last stock out of 6,000 to move up. **It will be a dog.** The investor will watch the share price remain where it is while everything else begins to move. The dog will not provide any price appreciation. Other opportunities will be missed if you are holding a dog for a month or two. Don't hang on to misery! Sell the dog. Take the loss.

If a company drops fifty percent in share price **in the first two years of an economic expansion** there could be several reasons.

- The product is not competitively priced.
- The product is no longer desirable.
- High operating, manufacturing and administrative expenses.

- Not a durable product.
- Old inefficient plant.
- Old inefficient management.
- Low worker wages.
- Poor employee work.
- Too large to operate efficiently.
- Can not meet a bond obligation at the bond's maturity date (or other current liability).
- Accidents and loss of property.
- Lawsuits and product liability.

A corporation that can not meet a bond obligation at the bond's maturity date is a corporation that has a financial problem. This is a corporation that is in trouble no matter how big or what wonderful product it produces.

If the company can arrange a satisfactory agreement with the bond holders to use common shares in an amount equivalent to make up for the lack of cash payment to the holders of a bond or a note due (or another arrangement), then they have dodged a bullet temporarily.

Now it is your turn!

You are the one who must become pro active. Immerse yourself in this environment. **You** must become the one to *explore the pathways*. **You** must become the one to *make the discovery.*

The disaster environment is the ideal time for you to profit. Once potential and novice investors have witnessed a steep decline in stock prices first hand, then they are in agreement to buy stocks at the bottom of the market.

You should be more than agreeable. Your main agenda should be to explore a steep market decline and experience the environment of the bottom of the market.

Throw away the channel changer and the action games. Leave that stale environment. The TV is only going to burn out on you and you with it. Instead of watching a dreary Reality TV show, pick up the phone and pursue your entry into the world of wealth. Empower yourself to make decisions to bring you wealth instead of which channel or movie to watch.

Before you put this book down call and open a **free** account. Take the first step. You will be amazed. Pick up the yellow pages. Look up stockbrokers and find a discount broker (Charles Schwab, AmeriTrade, E Trade, Scott Trade).

Find a corner in one room to set up a strategy table. You will feel good about yourself when you get to this point. Order the Securities Research Company Orange Book. Between the front and back cover 1500 graphs await your scrutiny. This book will be an inspiration. The first day you look at the graphs you will find more than ten companies that will keep you moving forward with your new endeavor.

In thirty days you will have one to five shares in five companies in different industries. Eventually you will become comfortable with this ongoing learning experience. Thirty days pass. Six months pass. Move from novice to beginner and on to intermediate. Make a one hundred and eighty degree turn in your active financial life.

Become involved and excited one day at a time. You will be able to answer the questions "What should I do next?" or "What needs to be done?" This is called problem solving. It does not matter that you do not have the solution immediately. Think about it. You will figure out a couple of alternative views or solutions. Answers will come to you the next day or two.

College and Trade schools will get you a job. To find wealth you must educate yourself. Only your own drive, your own will and desire and your own dogged pursuit will bring you wealth.

IN SUMMARY

Order the Orange book from Securities Research Company.

Read the Dead Cat Bounce two more times.

You know the basic characteristics of the market now. Watch the market every week. In the new market cycle from the low point, the market will rise for one to three years. It can rise for five, but this does not happen often.

Watch the market and your favorite stocks. Pay attention to quarterly earnings announcements and watch the stock price reaction.

Make your own guess at the high point that the Dow Jones Industrials will reach this current cycle. Monitor the earnings reports of your five favorite companies every quarter. While earnings advance or hold the market will do the same.

Call these five companies and ask them to mail a free copy of their annual report to you.

The newspapers will be all aglow about the DOW JONES new high and say that the economy is recovering or setting new records. This lasts for about a year or as little as six months. Then the first large downturn will appear. Companies can see 40 or 50 percent drops at this slide, but this is not yet the disaster area at the very bottom of the market.

There will be downward slides and they will be followed by rallies with the DOW climbing back.

The bottom of the market will be approximately two years later. This will be the big blow out with the dead cat bounce. It will last at least six months.

The signs that show that the market is weakening are as follows:.

- The quarterly report figures for earnings per share, operating income, sales, and net income are lower than the estimates made for the quarter. These quarterly figures will continue to be lower than expected.
- Consumer spending will be less as Americans tighten their belts. Employers will reduce working hours and eliminate second shifts. There will be layoffs and early retirement.
- Discount sales will be everywhere.
- Factory orders will be lower. There will be operating losses for the quarter. There will be declining sales. There will be downsizing. Growth will be non-existent. There will be plant closures
- Finally, before the big slide, there will be no gains in earnings for the quarter, but there will be no losses either. These quarters will be followed by quarters that have losses and negative earnings reports. The most common quote you will hear will hear will be…"Hold onto your stocks. Don't sell them. They will recover in the long run."

Then the big slide will begin. There will be a couple of days that the market will be closed. The sheer volume of selling orders will be too much for the floor brokers and the exchanges to handle.

Disaster Day is here! You will have six intense months to watch for your bargain basement prices.

Remember to mark your buy orders or your sell orders as Market Orders. "Buy at the market" or "sell at the market." You will not get the exact price that you see when you place the order. The price will be a little bit lower if you are selling. Likewise the price will be a little bit higher if you are buying. The most important outcome here is that your order will be filled immediately when received. You will not miss the chance to buy or sell. You will get the trade. If you miss this chance, then all of your time and effort has been wasted.

Good till cancelled orders and buy or sell limit orders will not always be honored or completed/filled no matter how long ago they were submitted to the brokerage house.

During severe market downturns and free falls, the markets are not orderly. They are highly volatile. The trading is erratic. You must use market orders to ensure that your order is honored.

APPENDIX

YOUR HOME MORTGAGE

Somewhere around the age of forty many of us become complacent with what we have. We no longer push ourselves or work as hard. Our attitudes and work ethic begin to fade along with our hopes and dreams. We decide to take the take the middle of the road and we begin to coast. **My friend, do not become complacent.** Trust me. This is not a good idea. When you chose to ignore the next economic downturn, then you have unconsciously chosen to ignore inflation. There is always a downturn in the economy and the markets for whatever reasons, lurking in the future. The inflation that is associated with market downturns will set you back. Over the long run these inflations will lower your standard of living. You must constantly save your money or buy a small plot of land or participate in stock market fire sale shopping. A hobby that you enjoy that produces income would be wonderful.

One way to save and invest easily is to forego the purchase of a new car. Use the$20,000 or $30,000 you will make in payments and buy two or four $5000 parcels of land instead. Then go to the local auto auction and buy a decent running car for less than $3000. Your insurance and plate taxes on the vehicle will be much lower. At the end of ten years your vehicles will have no value, but your land will have value and they might be paid for! You have to figure out what you are going to do to keep inflation from blowing your financial house away.

At the age of fifty, your burdens include more variables. You may not want to work as hard. Financially, the kids and the grand children need your help now and then. If the house is not paid off, you realize that you will be working full time to the age of sixty five and beyond.

If the mortgage was refinanced to pay off credit cards and other expenses, then the monthly payments are twice as high as the original payments. If you are a victim in the next collapsed economy and are laid off from the job, then you may go into foreclosure on the mortgage and lose the house.

The appreciation in the value of the home will disappear along with more than **one third of your monthly income for the last twenty years**. This is a heartbreaker! Mortgage companies (subsidiaries of big banks) do not give credit for twenty years of loyalty. They merely put you into foreclosure. What a terrible time to realize that you will not be able to retire before the age of seventy. You will find out how much more difficult it is to find a job in your new status as a senior citizen. Life is truly wonderful but financially there are struggles all along the way.

Make no mistake about it. The home is the most important investment.

The safest financial investment you can make is to pay down a thirty year mortgage in fifteen years. **This is an important concept**. To pay off the house in fifteen years is a terrific savings plan. You realize a savings of approximately ninety thousand dollars or more in mortgage interest on a one hundred and fifty thousand dollar house. Think of it as making ten times your money over ten years on a $9,000 investment in the stock market. An **amortization book,** with tables of five to sixteen percent, will clearly illustrate the savings in much greater payments towards the principle (paying off the loan amount) and much lower payments to interest (part of the agreement to finance the loan).

Remember, if the house is paid off, then you can survive a job lay off. You can take a lower paying job and still survive financially. You will not lose the house or have to sell it. If the value of the home goes down, **who cares**? It is paid for! You can live for free! No one believes they will ever experience a job lay off, especially during a long deep recession. In fact, this can happen to anyone during their thirties, forties and fifties.

Visualize paying down the principle balance on the home three thousand to five thousand dollars every year! Watch your hard earned money pay down more of the loan principle every month.

Does this mean that you have to give up the retirement account?

If the chart of your employer's stock has a lack luster performance and there is nothing hot in the company hopper, then the answer is yes. Yes, for the simple reason that if the house is not paid off in thirty years, then it will break your financial back. Get the house paid off! You won't see thirty percent of your paycheck going to the mortgage company every month for half of your life. Afterward, you can open an IRA.

If your employer has a retirement plan you will be asked to view the power point presentation. You may be in a group of recently hired workers. The presentation will introduce the IRA plan. The usual presentation will explain when and how much the company will contribute to the retirement account. The company stock may be offered at a price lower than it currently trades on the open market. Your monetary contribution of $1,000 to $5,000 is usually converted to shares of company stock at a discount price. In later years your contribution is matched to some degree by the company. This seems to be an excellent compensation.

A form letter is passed around to be filled out. You are supposed to indicate how much money you want to contribute to the IRA account from the monthly paycheck.

Now is the time to be bold. Be audacious. Tell the host that you are planning on making a $5,000 payment to reduce the principle amount of the home mortgage this year. Ask the host if the company will match fifty percent of this principle reduction payment that you will make on the home mortgage.

Tell them you prefer to pay down the mortgage because there is **no risk**. The dollar amounts are set in stone and the hard earned money is not subject to the drifting prices of the stock market. Currently, there are a few companies that participate in mortgage reduction programs. They match your payment by a percentage and the popularity of this program is increasing.

The employer may argue that the value of the home may decrease. It is up to you to remind them of three things.

- If the house is paid off, then you can live there for free and have all of the money from the monthly paycheck.
- Remind them that you will save ninety thousand dollars if you pay the mortgage off in fifteen years.
- Remind them that you can not live under a pile of worthless stock certificates.

The host may look at you as if you are crazy. He or she may perform an impressive tap dance of double talk and gibberish. This dance is designed to overcome the objections and distract you.

Then the spokesperson will ask intimidating questions linked to high finance. Basically, they believe that the company stock will never go down.

The best answer to these intimidating financial questions should be, "Will it save me ninety thousand dollars? Will you put that in writing?"

If the host dances away from the original question by changing the subject, or if he expresses a look of shock or anger, then speak up and remind him in a loud voice that, "**Debt is the most common failure to the individual!**"

If you are so lucky as to be in a dynamic company and the stock is on its way to the moon, then leave the stock in the retirement account. **If the stock is a dog in the doldrums, then sell it and leave the proceeds in the account for a better opportunity.**

Never stop learning and never give up. *You are going to learn how to build your financial wealth and not lose it.*

YOUR IRA OR KEOGH

The IRA and KEOGH company power point presentation. Looks pretty good, doesn't it? The price to pay for shares of company stock in the IRA may be lower than the current market price. This is one way that the company is able to compensate you for your good hard work.

Management believes the price of their stock will continue to climb in the long run. Play along with them. Graphs over long periods of time give the impression that the market is always going up. The small downturns appear to be only a temporary setback. Rest assured, the small downturns were due to recessions or a decrease in company production. **Rest assured that the share price of the company stock took a nose dive at that time.**

The company may offer extra stock because you have been a conscientious worker for more than five years. If the time and price happens to be in Area B, **then you will be a winner!**

The company will have an in house retirement plan department or an arrangement with a securities representative or a consultant. Contact this entity and check to make certain that you have control of buying and selling in your account.

If you are in Area D then sell the shares and leave the cash proceeds in the account. If it is a large amount of money, then take the money out and pay down the home mortgage. There will be an early withdraw penalty. The prepaid penalty will be easily made up by **the reduction of the heavy interest payments on the mortgage principle.** The day you do not have to send **one third of your monthly income** to the mortgage company **will arrive ten years early.**

This action would be preferable to holding the stock during a two year market decline. Who wants to watch stock in a retirement account sink fifty percent in value over two years?

What if the IRA is up to eighty thousand dollars from the contributions for the last ten to fifteen years and then the stock **collapses fifty percent?** You will never make up this loss. This is poor investing, and you lost with hard earned money. What could be worse? Seventy five percent would be worse.

You are responsible for your gain. Lock in the gain. Sell! Call the portfolio manager and convert the shares to cash! The only way to realize profit in an IRA or a mutual fund is to sell before the value drops. If the business cycle has expanded two years and right now the GDP/GNP/the economy and the stock market are going sideways and slipping down, then sell. Do this **because you are a winner**. Do not listen to other people's baloney or hang along for the ride. "Suffer no fools." If the stock continues to go up, there will always be another time.

Count on a stock market collapse in the fourth year **maybe** *seventy percent of the time*. If it does not happen in the fourth year it will by the sixth.

Is it better to invest in the stock market, the IRA, or the home mortgage? Which is more important?

They are all important. The main point here is that the money is hard earned money. Your hard earned money should not be lost in a stock market gamble.

If the employer stock falls fifteen to twenty five percent, an analyst for the company may print up a recommendation not to sell the stock. "Hold on to the stock. In the long run the stock will recover! The stock will outperform the competition. Good news is coming!"

A month later the analyst will announce some dreary little news that is common knowledge and the stock price will remain at the same level.

After two years of reading recommendations and research one understands that "Hold" means that **the stock is a dog**. "Hold" is the hope and the wish that the share price will rebound for you, but first, investors more important than you (brokerage firms and mutual funds) need to sell (dump) their holdings in the stock before you do so.

If there is an impending across the board economic downturn, sell the shares. If you are a millionaire, then hang on. If you were not losing your job and going into foreclosure you could hang on.

If the company is leading the competition in sales of gizmos the investment might be safe. The share price will recover, but you really need to find out the reasons that the stock is low to make an informed decision.

Management may talk about insider trading. They will say in some situations you may not be able to sell the shares in the IRA account.

These announcements will cause a company stock to rise.

- A lucrative contract.
- A large increase in net earnings or revenues.
- A pending merger.
- An acquisition.

- An announcement of a miracle cure.
- An announcement of a new product that will beat the competition.

If you have knowledge of such information and pass this to an individual who does not, then you may become part of the violation. The general public does not have access to this information.

If the individual buys the shares before the announcement and then sells them at a profit after the stock moves up, then they have benefited monetarily. The general public has not.

This chain of events is known as insider trading and both people are guilty at any point in the process.

Otherwise, sell the employee shares anytime you wish.

The concept of IRA and the Keogh plans was designed to encourage people to increase their savings and invest for their retirement. The plans were enacted into law through congress with good intentions. Hopefully, it would be a solution to **the coming social security crisis.** More people could manage their own retirement and their employers could help. Imagine if companies and individuals no longer had to pay social securities taxes.

What a sales job! The obvious hurdle here is that there are not enough wins for every single person to benefit. Obviously, everyone who owns a home can benefit by paying down the principle balance on the mortgage. The house may not be your dream home, but you have to appreciate what you have.

Stocks do not always go up. Citigroup employee retirement plans were at an all time low in 2009. The employees at Enron lost all of the value in their retirement shares.

Retirement shares at banks that have closed are worthless. Bank shares that have dropped from $20 a share to $3 have lost the worker's hard earned money.

If you want to find out why banks loan all of the interest payments from home and commercial loans in the USA to other nations in the world, then read two books by Paul Erdman.

Paul Erdman was born in Canada. He became an American citizen and a banker in the state of California. He was the first American to open the very first American bank in Switzerland. He has five international bestsellers to his credit, and these books will open your eyes and shed a little light on the shenanigans that can take place in the banking industry. After all, the banks do own most of the commercial and residential mortgages as well as the mortgage companies in America.

Paul was "caught with his fingers in the till." He used the money in customer accounts at the bank as collateral so he could trade currency futures and coffee futures. "The Crash of '79" and "The Panic of '89" are two of his best books.

Obviously, the main attraction of the IRA or Keogh is the capital gains income tax advantage. **There are no taxes on the gains made in the stock market in the IRA or Keogh account.** The tax exempt ploy was used deliberately to influence individuals to consider the retirement plans. Government and financial securities companies sometimes have a slick way of selling ideas to the public. Consumer decisions are influenced if government makes something taxable or tax exempt.

Regardless, everyone hopped on the retirement wagon!

MUTUAL FUNDS

Here is a brief summary of the last 40 years of mutual fund history. The following figures are approximate. They are not exact.

In 1969 there were 250 mutual funds in the USA. After the market crash in 1970 there were 25 mutual funds that survived the crash. The others closed up shop as fast as ice cream melts on a hot summer day.

In 1977 there were approximately 2500 mutual funds. After the market crash in 1978 there were 250 mutual funds that were financially sound and able to continue in business.

Today there are over 30,000 mutual funds in the world.

The mutual fund expansion began after the IRA and Keogh plans became law. Mutual funds became the preferred investment vehicle for retirement accounts.

Investors wanted an investment method that would bring them some worthwhile gains rather than the meager money market profits. Self employed individuals looked to mutual funds for their retirement accounts. It was considered the astute thing to do. A team of knowledgeable professionals could increase your wealth.

Your money is in the hands of professional managers. Some of them are armed with the most analytical software programs in the world. You can relax. You do not have to be directly involved with the trading decisions. The fund managers buy and sell stocks to increase the value of the fund. Their gains are reflected by the increase in the value of your fund shares. Sit back and watch the investment grow. Ride it all the way to the top of the market **and then make a decision to sell.** Mutual funds do not magically continue to rise. Mutual funds are subject to the same uncertainties and market fluctuations as shares of company stock.

The share value is the current price you will receive **if you sell the shares.** Profit is not "realized" or "locked in" until the shares are sold. **You are responsible** to contact the mutual fund account representative or your company's sponsor. The fund shares must be sold to realize the gain.

After the 2009 crash a few funds are up as much as two hundred percent within a year (Goldman Sachs). Astute managers who anticipated the downturn sold part of the fund's investments (hopefully at a profit) to raise cash prior to the **market crash.** Then they **waited for the thin ice to break, and they went fire sale shopping**.

If you invest in a mutual fund do some homework. Check the reputation and the credentials of the fund and the managers. Forbes magazine rates the performance of the top mutual funds. You can find a copy of this magazine at any large library in their magazine section or the financial reference book section.

Exercise some care if you select a mutual fund. If there is a corruption factor of one percent or more in the industry, then three hundred funds out of thirty thousand may be fraudulent. Everyone has heard of Bernie Madoff. There are pyramid schemes in the world to steal your money.

The account executives are perceived as knowledgeable veterans of the stock market. They appear to be confident survivors of the last market calamity. They have a propensity to brag and swagger. They have plenty of hot air to blow up pants and skirts.   " O u r funds have returned seventeen percent every year for the last five years. It will pay for the children's college education. We are ranked in the top twenty five mutual funds in the nation and the top fifty in the world. We have conservative funds. We have highly diversified funds. We have businessman's risk funds and world growth funds." They add with a whisper, "Our funds gained more than ten percent in the last market crash."

Account executives believe the fund value will never go down.

ABOUT THE AUTHOR

Bill Overmyer worked as a stockbroker in Denver, Colorado. He witnessed three devastating market downturns. After several attempts to share his experience with potential investors he decided to write an easily understood guide that would lead a new investor safely through the paths of a stock market disaster. Bill lives in Colorado where he enjoys camping and skiing in the Rocky Mountains.

Author of *Bronze Miner.*